Anyone can do it.
But it helps to be a little crazy.
You climb a high tower or crane.
Or perhaps you go up in a hot-air balloon.
In any case, someone attaches
a thick rubber band around your ankles.
Then you leap out into the wild blue yonder.

A bungee jumper in the South Pacific.

Bungee Jumping

Henry Billings and Melissa Billings

Published in association with The Basic Skills Agency

Hodder & Stoughton

A MEMBER OF THE HODDER HEADLINE GROUP

Acknowledgements

Cover: Craig Lovell/Corbis.

Photos: p. 2 © James Davis Travel Photography, p. 5 Solo Syndication Ltd,
pp. 12, 16, 19, 23, 26 © Action-Plus Photographic

Orders: please contact Bookpoint Ltd, 39 Milton Park, Abingdon, Oxon OX14 4TD. Telephone: (44) 01235 400414, Fax: (44) 01235 400454. Lines are open from 9.00–6.00, Monday to Saturday, with a 24 hour message answering service. Email address: orders@bookpoint.co.uk

British Library Cataloguing in Publication Data
A catalogue record for this title is available from The British Library

ISBN 0 340 74718 8

Published by Jamestown Publishers,
a division of NTC/Contemporary Publishing Group, Inc.

Copyright © 1996 by NTC/Contemporary Publishing Group, Inc.

First published in UK 1999 by Hodder & Stoughton Educational Publishers.
Impression number   10 9 8 7 6 5 4 3
Year   2004 2003 2002 2001 2000 1999

Typeset by Fakenham Photosetting Ltd, Fakenham, Norfolk.
Printed in Great Britain for Hodder & Stoughton Educational, a division of Hodder Headline Plc, 338 Euston Road, London NW1 3BH by Redwood Books, Trowbridge, Wiltshire.

Your body plunges towards the earth below.
Then, at the last moment,
the rubber band stops you.
This is not your day to die.

The sport is called bungee jumping.
It began long ago on certain islands
in the South Pacific.
Each spring the islanders gathered vines
They wove them into a kind of rope.

Then young men called 'land divers'
climbed high towers.
They tied the vines to their ankles
and jumped.

They did it to prove their courage.
A good jump was also supposed
to help ensure* healthy crops for the island.

* to help ensure means to make certain of getting

The first bungee jumper in England jumped from a high bridge.

Modern bungee jumping began in England
on 1 April 1979.
Note the day.
It was April Fool's Day.

The members of the
Oxford Dangerous Sports Club
were looking for a new thrill.

They had heard of 'land diving'
and wanted to try it for themselves.
So the men climbed up a high bridge,
tied rubber ropes to their ankles,
and jumped.
One member later said the jump was
really quite pleasurable.

But it was a man from New Zealand
who made bungee jumping a big sport.
His name was Alan John Hackett.

Hackett was quite a daredevil.
He had once jumped off the Eiffel Tower
in Paris, France.

Alan John Hackett gets ready to jump.

In 1988, he wanted to give others
a chance to try bungee jumping.
At this time, though, the sport was illegal.
So Hackett made a deal
with the New Zealand police.
Using his own money,
he would mend an old bridge
over a river gorge.
In return, the police let him open
a legal bungee jumping centre on the bridge.

The centre was a huge success.
Hackett gave each jumper a special T-shirt.
It became very popular among daredevils.
Everyone wanted one of those shirts.
And since the only way to get one
was to make a jump,
more and more people agreed to do it.

A bungee jumper heads for the river.

Some jumpers did really wild things.
They asked to jump with an extra long rope.
That way they would dip into the river
before the rope pulled them back.
One man put shampoo on his head.
When he bounced up out of the water,
he was washing his hair!

Bungee jumping soon caught on in America.
At first, only the boldest people did it.
But over time others joined in.
All kinds of people took the plunge.
Even one man who was helped
out of a wheelchair jumped.
And no jumpers complained
about having to pay to do it.

As thrills go,
it is hard to beat bungee jumping.
The platforms used for the jumps
are ten floors high, or higher.
That means jumpers fall as far as
50 metres before the rope saves them.
First-time jumpers can almost taste
their fear.

The first jump can be terrifying.

One man thought about it for a year
before he jumped.
He said his palms began to sweat
just thinking about it.
A young girl said she was terrified
the first time she jumped.
Another said her terror was
cold and rippling.

Some jumpers make jokes
to calm their nerves.
One woman was asked how old she was,
just before she jumped.
She said she hoped to be 29 soon.

Most jumpers are young, but some are not.
One man made his first leap
at the age of 100.

Bungee jumpers can be any age.

There is, of course, real danger.
You have to be very careful
when bungee jumping.
One mistake, and you're history.
And while most people live to tell the tale,
a few don't.

In 1989, two French jumpers died
when their ropes broke.
A third died when he fell and hit a tower.

In 1991, the first American jumper died
when his rope came undone
as he leapt through the air.

So accidents do happen.
But for many,
the danger just adds to the excitement.
Besides, bungee jumpers don't talk
about the accidents.
They talk about the successes.
They talk about facing their fears.
And they talk about
the joy of the fall itself.

A bungee jumper bounces like a yo-yo.

During a jump,
a person hits speeds of 60 miles an hour.
Then, when the rope tightens,
the jumper springs back up into the air
like a rocket.
For a short time,
he or she is like a human yo-yo,
bouncing up and down in the breeze.
When the rope loses its bounce,
the ride is over.

Even then, though, some of the joy remains.
Jumpers feel both happy and relieved
when it is over.
Most laugh and smile
as they are unhooked from the rope.
Many of them shout

Hey, look at me.
I did it!

The thrill of the jump.

It is, as one person said,
a natural high.
Bungee jumpers even have a name
for this soaring feeling.
They call it the post-bungee grin.

Maybe some day you will decide
to make that leap of faith
and share that grin.
All it takes is a little money
and a lot of nerve.